Read and Rhyme LEVEL 2 ★★

Ship Trip

by Pearl Markovics

Consultant:
Beth Gambro
Reading Specialist
Yorkville, Illinois

Contents

BEARPORT PUBLISHING

New York, New York

Ship Trip

Let's rhyme!

This is **Chip**.

Chip is on a **ship**.

He tries to **skip**.

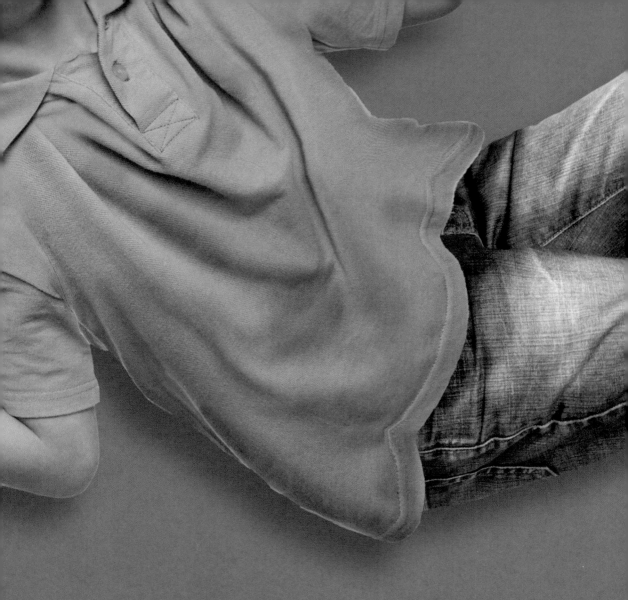

Chip slips.
He falls on his **hip**.

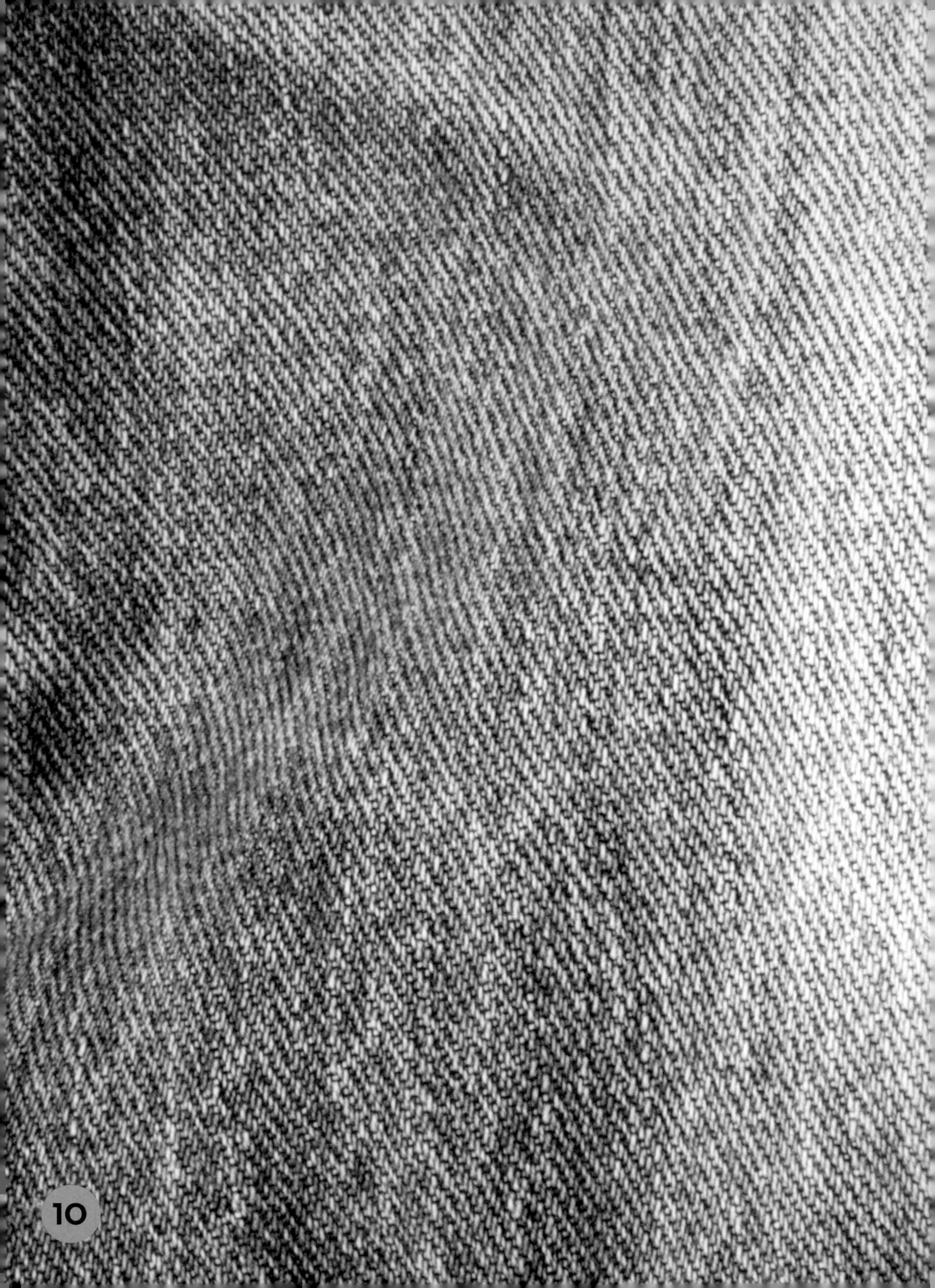

Then, his
pants **rip**.

Chip bites his **lip.**

This is not a fun **trip**.

Key Words in the **-ip** Family

hip

lip

rip

ship

skip

trip

Other **-ip** Words: **dip, flip, grip**

Index

About the Author

Pearl Markovics enjoys having fun with words. She especially likes witty wordplay.

16